CW01560481

SPEAK-OLOGY

How to Speak with Confidence, Fluency &
Eloquence. Fluent Speaking Skills & Smart
Language for Highly Effective Communication

+349 Expert Speaking Templates, Phrases &
Idioms for Professional Communication in English

Business English Originals ©

www.macsonbell.com

By **Marc Roche**

Language Specialist & Executive Coach

Copyright 2023 Marc Roche

Macson Bell ® Business & Law

http://www.macsonbell.com/

Topics Covered in this communication book:

Effective communication book: how to speak eloquently, the power of words, effective speaking, how highly effective people speak, speaking books, English pronunciation book, books on communication, speak English fluently, speak English, books to learn English.

Contents

PRIVATE LIBRARY ACCESS

Get the FREE Books + Training using the
Private Executive Club link at the back of this book.

English as the Language of International Work and Business

In the professional world, distinctions between global and local languages are becoming increasingly pronounced. As economies intertwine and borders blur in the business and legal sectors, English has emerged as the predominant lingua franca. It's not merely a convenient tool; it's a critical asset for those wishing to be at the forefront of their fields. From boardrooms in Tokyo to after-work cocktails in Barcelona, the resonating echoes of English conversations mark the pulse of global commerce.

However, it's not just about speaking English; it's about mastering it. As international collaboration continues to grow, it's no longer enough to be average at communicating—you need to be a confident, articulate, and culturally aware communicator. It's no longer enough to understand and be understood; professionals must also appreciate the subtleties and nuances of high-stakes and cross-cultural communication. In global contexts, misunderstandings can be costly, and opportunities can be missed due to subtle misinterpretations.

This shift isn't isolated to the boardrooms of large corporations and international law firms. Small businesses, freelancers, and even students find themselves in an environment where they regularly interact with peers from around the globe. Digital platforms and remote work have further accentuated this trend, making it almost commonplace to hold a video conference with participants from multiple continents.

Education systems and professional training modules are recognizing this evolution, but many are still stuck in the past. This book aims to contribute to a generation of professionals who are technically sound, linguistically agile, and culturally smart.

In the following pages, we will explore the dynamics of this transformation, diving deep into the intricacies of English as the cornerstone of international business and law. We will understand its nuances and, most importantly, equip you with the tools to excel in this globalized landscape.

The right words said in the right way can change everything.

The Challenge

Cultural Sensitivities: Beyond language, understanding the myriad of cultural references, idioms, and other non-verbal signals is a significant challenge. These often get lost in translation, leading to misinterpretations.

Educational Infrastructure: Many regions might not have the infrastructure or resources to provide advanced training. Even where facilities exist, the quality of training might vary, leading to inconsistent proficiency levels.

Digital Divide: The increasing reliance on digital platforms for global communication emphasizes the importance of technological literacy alongside linguistic proficiency. Not everyone has equal access to technology or the skills to use it effectively.

Rapidly Evolving Business Jargon: The world of international business and law is dynamic, with new terminologies, slang, and jargon emerging frequently.

This ever-evolving vocabulary is a challenge, even for native speakers.

Cost Implications: High-quality training programs, especially those focusing on cultural communication and language, can be expensive. This can limit access for many who need it.

Evaluation Metrics: Measuring proficiency in speaking and communication isn't just about grammar and vocabulary tests. Assessing cultural understanding and the ability to navigate cross-cultural scenarios effectively is far more complex.

Scalability: Given the sheer number of professionals requiring this training, providing individualized, effective training at scale becomes a formidable challenge.

Only by recognizing and confronting these hurdles can we hope to serve the growing need for fluent, confident, and culturally aware communication in international business and law.

About this Book

Designed for both native and advanced non-native English speakers, this book provides a comprehensive guide to mastering the art of professional spoken communication.

Speak-ology: How to Speak with Confidence, Fluency & Eloquence +349 Expert Speaking Templates, Phrases & Idioms for Professional Communication in English, provides a comprehensive framework under which both native and advanced non-native English speakers can significantly improve their speaking skills for professional settings.

Readers will engage in targeted speaking and language activities aimed at enhancing their linguistic prowess and boosting their overall competence and confidence in diverse professional environments.

At the end of the book, you'll discover an amazing collection of *349 Expert Speaking Templates and Phrases* that guide you through the language of leadership, delivering speeches, presentations, pitches, starting conversations at work, idioms, and other forms of professional communication.

Who is this book for?

Designed for both native and advanced non-native English speakers, this book provides a comprehensive guide to mastering professional communication.

Does the book contain exercises for self-study, or is it for classroom learning?

You can use *Speak-ology* for self-training or in the classroom. The book contains deep knowledge, clearly explained strategies, tools, and speaking and communication exercises under the "Training" sections.

Is this book suitable for non-native English (ESL) speakers?

Yes. Speak-ology is written for both native and non-native English speakers. A non-native English speaker will need a C1 or C2 (Advanced) level under the CEFR (Common European Framework of Reference for Languages) to properly follow the information and materials.

Is this book appropriate for NATIVE English speakers?

Yes. Absolutely. The book is designed for native and non-native English-speaking professionals. It is packed with specialized language and communication training to help native-English speakers master professional communication.

What Makes *Speak-ology* Different?

Many speaking books and courses focus on presentation or body language tricks. However, they ignore the crucial role of clear thinking and precise language. It is like trying to build a house by decorating the roof before laying the foundation—it doesn't work.

Since 2013, our courses and private coaching sessions have employed the strategies in this book to help thousands of professionals master language and communication for international business and work. Whether you're an instructor teaching a class or an individual pursuing self-development, this book offers a structured path.

What will I learn?

 Inside This Speaking & Effective Communication Book:

- ✓ Discover **the Power of Words.**
- ✓ Master Clear Thinking and **Language for Impactful Communication**.
- ✓ Learn to Structure Your Thoughts for **Effective Speaking.**
- ✓ Learn to **speak fluently** with strategic exercises.
- ✓ Learn **how to be more articulate** in every conversation.
- ✓ Explore **how to be eloquent** and transmit unmatched confidence.
- ✓ Use our detailed **English pronunciation chart** for flawless speech.
- ✓ **Speak with Full Confidence:** Learn **how highly effective people speak** and mimic their techniques.
- ✓ Achieve **Clarity and Respect in Professional Conversations.**
- ✓ Learn How to Create **Powerful Descriptions** for **Impactful Communication.**
- ✓ Discover how to make your message memorable.
- ✓ Improve **your communication** for **effective workplace conversations.**
- ✓ Learn How to **Answer Difficult Questions** like an expert.
- ✓ How to **Transform Serious Mistakes into Career Victories.**

- ✓ Includes Video Training on **Expert Breathing Techniques for Effective Speaking.**
- ✓ Unlock the **7 Communication Habits of Highly Effective Teams.**
- ✓ Learn **Active Listening Techniques.**
- ✓ Includes **349 Expert Speaking Templates, Phrases, and Idioms for Professional Communication in English.**

Where can I find the Special Phrases and Idioms?

You can **download the resources** and access **FREE training** using the **Executive Club** link at the back of the book.

Chapter 1: Introduction- Clear Thinking is the Engine of Effective Communication.

Master clear thinking & language for impactful communication

In the world of communication, clarity is key. Your thinking guides your words and confidence levels to ensure your message is effectively understood. Hence, your thoughts must be clear before you can speak them effectively.

If you can master clear thinking and clear language, you can be an exceptional speaker. This book teaches you exactly how to do that. Body language, eye contact, and all other communication elements will fall into place naturally once you master your thinking and language. This is the method that every great speaker throughout history has used.

The Fluency Cycle

Excellent communication is more than stringing words together; it's a cycle of understanding, articulating, and refining your thoughts and ideas. In the next few chapters, we will introduce and guide you through the "Fluency Cycle" concept.

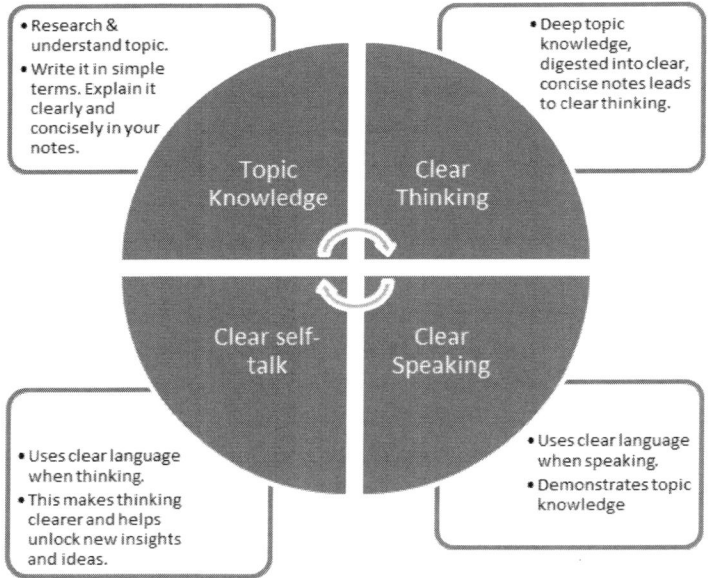

1) Topic Knowledge: First, you research your topic, make notes, and ensure you fully understand it. You can't talk effectively about subjects you know nothing about.

2) Clear Thinking: Deep topic knowledge and applying clear, concise language leads to clear thinking.

3) Clear Speaking: Once you have a deep understanding of the subject, you've expressed it clearly in writing, and you've achieved clear thinking about the topic; this leads to effective speaking.

4) Clear Self-Talk: After this, practicing clear language during self-talk and analysis of the topic makes thinking even clearer and helps unlock new and original insights and ideas. You will get better and better; as long as you continue the cycle, it never ends.

This *Fluency Cycle* is the basis of highly effective communication. All other factors are supplementary and come as a result of practicing this cycle. Without a solid foundation in these elements, long-term improvement in communication is difficult.

Zettelkasten Method: The Straightforward Guide

Alright, let's dive into the Zettelkasten note-taking method. It's a smart system that organizes all those buzzing ideas in your head.

Here's how to do it:

1. Quick Scribbles:

Anytime an idea comes up, write it down. It could be on sticky notes, a notebook, or your preferred digital app. These are your "fleeting notes."

2. Idea Clean-Up:

After you've got some rest, revisit those fleeting notes. Throw away what doesn't resonate and expand on the most valuable ideas. Imagine it's a little like decluttering your desk.

3. The 3-2-1 Approach (for each idea):

Write three key points about your idea.

Trim it to two standout ideas.

Choose the top one, giving it a more detailed explanation. This is your "literature note."

4. Solidifying Ideas:

From your literature notes, draft "permanent notes." Aim for clarity and ensure each note captures a single thought.

5. Streamline and Connect:

Break down your ideas to their essence in a clear sentence. Every note should have an easy-to-remember identifier (like a catchy tag or number). Link related notes to create a smooth flow of ideas.

6. Regular Refresh:

Revisit your notes occasionally. Update where needed and add new links. It's like updating your professional portfolio – but for ideas.

7. Embrace the Growth:

As you add and link more notes, your knowledge grows. It's not just about writing things down; it's about making meaningful connections and having a growing bank of knowledge.

The Twitter Test: From Deep Knowledge to Key Messages

A useful technique for improving your key messages is the "Twitter Test." The premise is simple: If you can't condense your key message into a tweet of 280 characters, it's not focused enough.

By putting your key messages through the Twitter Test, you ensure you and your audience can understand your main points quickly and easily. This is crucial whether you're trying to educate trainees, convince stakeholders in a meeting, deliver a memorable conference presentation, or negotiate a deal.

Remember, the Zettelkasten Method equips you with deep and interconnected knowledge, but it's through clear, concise key messages that this knowledge can make a real impact. So, don't stop at understanding—hone your message and watch your influence grow.

Worksheet

If you can't condense your key message into a tweet (280 characters, or around 70 words), it's not refined enough. Use the following process whenever you need to prepare for an important conversation.

Step 1- Identify Your Key Messages: After researching and refining your notes, write your most important messages below. We've used three key messages in this exercise.

a. Message 1:

_____

b. Message 2:

_____

c. Message 3:

_____

Step 2- Refine: Now that you have written your key messages in the previous section, use this section to compress each message. Write each message in 70 words or less.

a. Tweet Version of Key Message 1 (maximum 70 words):

_____

b. Tweet Version of Key Message 2 (maximum 70 words):

_____

c. Tweet Version of Key Message 3 (maximum 70 words):

_____

Step 3- Final Key Messages (Twitter Test Approved): Is the message clear and concise? If not, refine it until it meets the word limit without losing its essence.

a. Key Message 1:

_____

b. Key Message 2:

_____

c. Key Message 3:

_____

Chapter 2. The 7 Rules of Fluency

Your words have the power to shape perceptions, so use them to build bridges, not walls.

Your fluency will be directly proportional to two crucial factors: your understanding of the subject matter, which we covered in the initial chapters, and your experience speaking about that knowledge. In other words, the best speakers are the readiest.

Generally speaking, fluency is a byproduct of preparation. Of course, innate talent can play a significant role, as in all skills, but as in all skills, you still need to encourage and train this inherent talent, or it will be useless. This also applies if you feel you're not naturally good at speaking. As we will see in this chapter, anyone can become a confident and fluent speaker with preparation.

Sir Winston Churchill, From Stutterer to Legendary Speaker

Throughout history, some people have risen above their limitations and defied the odds to leave a mark on the world. Winston Churchill was one of those people. But his path to becoming one of the most influential speakers in history was paved with obstacles.

Churchill's speech impediments, particularly his stutter and lisp, made it extremely difficult to express himself effectively initially. He faced ridicule and criticism, often being dismissed as inadequate. However, he refused to let his limitations define him.

Churchill understood that mastery of speaking required relentless practice. He diligently worked on his speech patterns, focusing on his delivery, tone, and cadence. By meticulously rehearsing his speeches, Churchill improved his ability to communicate with clarity and impact. Through countless hours of practice, he transformed his weaknesses into strengths.

Churchill's rise as one of history's greatest speakers was further bolstered by his unwavering leadership during World War II. At a time of immense crisis and uncertainty, his resolute spirit and rallying speeches united Britain. Despite his speaking problems, his speeches were legendary because he focused on the message. His message was the important part, not him, not his voice, not his lisp. Churchill's ability to inspire and motivate others through his message became a defining characteristic of his leadership.

Winston Churchill's journey from a stuttering and lisping speaker to one of the most influential speakers the world has ever seen is an extraordinary tale of triumph over adversity. Through relentless determination, meticulous practice, and unwavering leadership, he defied his natural limitations to become a powerful voice that inspired generations. Churchill's story reminds us that we can overcome our weaknesses as communicators with practice. His legacy inspires people worldwide, reminding us that greatness can emerge from even the humblest beginnings.

The greatest thing about his transformation from hopeless to legendary speaker is that his speech impediments did not go away. By increasing his fluency through relentless practice, his lisp and stutter became distinctive elements of his brand. It made him unique and even more inspiring. This is the power of fluency through practice. It brings out your uniqueness.

Apart from gathering, organizing, and structuring your ideas, your preparation should also involve constant practice. Don't feel discouraged if you initially stumble over your words and feel sluggish; it's normal. Fluency is a direct product of rehearsal. Practice focusing your thoughts only on your message while you speak.

So, remember, mastery requires practice, just like learning to play the piano. Over time, your fingers instinctively play the right notes. Similarly, as an untrained speaker, things may initially seem daunting. But with perseverance, you'll eventually find your rhythm. The flow of your speech will be as fluid as your practice.

Discussion Questions:

1. Personal Resilience:

Have you ever faced a personal limitation or challenge that you've had to overcome? What motivated you to push through it, and how did you do so?

2. Speech and Identity:

Do you think unique traits, like Churchill's lisp and stutter, can become distinctive and admirable aspects of someone's identity? Why or why not?

3. Defining Success:

Do you believe that success is measured by perfection or by progress? In Churchill's case, he didn't eliminate his speech impediments but learned to use them. How does this change or affirm your perception of success?

4. Message vs. Medium:

How important is the way a message is delivered compared to the content of the message itself? Can you think of modern examples where the content of a message was overshadowed by its delivery?

5. The Role of Persistence:

Churchill showed extreme persistence in the face of adversity. Do you think this quality is innate, or can it be developed? Can you share a personal experience where persistence led to a breakthrough?

The 7 Rules of Fluency

Rule 1- Overcoming Limitations: Despite his stutter and lisp, Churchill refused to let these limitations define him. This teaches us the importance of having the courage to face our challenges directly. Like Churchill, you may also have limitations that hinder your speaking abilities. Don't let these define you. Turn your challenges into opportunities, and let your struggles fuel your desire to improve.

Rule 2- The Power of Preparation: Churchill diligently improved his speaking, demonstrating that fluency often stems from extensive preparation and practice. Churchill's diligence is a lesson in the value of preparation. Commit yourself to investing time and energy in improving your speech. Plan, prepare, and rehearse your speeches. With each rehearsal, you'll find your fluency improving.

Rule 3- Turning Weaknesses into Strengths: Churchill turned his unique speech patterns into a signature part of his brand by focusing on his message. This shows us that perceived weaknesses can be transformed into unique strengths.

Use your perceived weaknesses to your advantage. Whether you are worried about your stutter, your accent, your body language, or anything else, you can use it to your advantage. Churchill turned his unique speech patterns into his signature style. You, too, can transform your weaknesses into unique strengths. Embrace your quirks and make them an integral part of your brand.

Rule 4- Staying Resilient During Difficult Times: Churchill's leadership during WWII showed his resilience. His ability to deliver compelling speeches under such pressure shows that fluency can be maintained even during difficult situations.

Life will throw challenges at you, which might shake your confidence. Take inspiration from Churchill's resilience. Hold on to your resolve, and let your words inspire others even during difficult times.

Rule 5- Importance of the Message: Remember, it's the message that counts. So, focus on the substance of your message. Deliver it with conviction and authenticity, and it will resonate with your audience.

Rule 6- Consistency in Practice: Mastering fluency is a long-term commitment requiring persistence. Churchill's path to fluency was paved with consistent practice. This is a clear reminder that there are no shortcuts to mastery. Stay committed to practicing your speaking skills regularly. Persistence is key, and over time, you will reap the benefits.

Rule 7- Transformation Through Practice: Everyone starts somewhere. Even Churchill was once an untrained speaker who struggled with his confidence. But with time, practice, and patience, he found his rhythm. So can you. Embrace the transformation journey and think of each time you practice as a small step towards becoming a more fluent speaker.

The Churchill Fluency Exercise

Here's a step-by-step activity to help you improve your speaking fluency. This process, over time, will build your confidence and improve your speaking fluency as you constantly practice and refine your speech.

Step 1: Set Clear Objectives

Before starting, define what you want to improve. Are you working on reducing filler words, speaking more clearly, or improving your pacing? Having clear objectives will guide your practice sessions.

Step 2: Pick a Topic

Choose a topic that you're passionate about. This will make the activity more enjoyable, and the words flow more easily.

Step 3: Research and Prepare

Do thorough research on the topic. This will give you a firm grasp of the subject matter, which will boost your confidence and help you speak more fluently.

Step 4: Draft a Speech

Write a short speech on the topic. This will help you organize your thoughts and create a logical flow to your presentation.

Step 5: Practice Out Loud

Practice your speech out loud. This will help you become familiar with how the words feel in your mouth and sound in your ears.

Step 6: Record Your Practice

Use your phone or a voice recorder to record your practice. This will allow you to listen to your speech and identify areas for improvement.

Step 7: Analyze and Adjust

Listen to your recording. Pay attention to your pacing, clarity, use of filler words, and pronunciation. Identify any parts of your speech where you stumble or lose fluency.

Step 8: Get Feedback

Share your recording with a trusted friend, family member, or mentor. Their feedback will provide an outside perspective on your fluency and overall delivery.

Step 9: Implement Changes

Based on your self-analysis and feedback, make necessary adjustments to your speech. This might mean rewriting parts, changing your pacing, or focusing on pronunciation.

Step 10: Repeat

Repeat the process until you're happy with your progress. Remember, improving speaking fluency is a long-term commitment requiring consistent practice.

Chapter 3. Achieving Clarity: Confidence & Respect in Professional Conversations

Without clear language, the deepest insight and wisdom can be mistaken for mere confusion; with it, even the simplest ideas can shine as brightly as stars.

The power of clear language is in its ability to make complex ideas understandable and accessible. It's akin to turning on a light in a dark room; suddenly, everything is visible and makes sense. Albert Einstein's scientific theories, undeniably complex, became known and understood worldwide thanks to his ability to explain them in simple, clear language.

Thoughts and words are closely linked. They interact and influence each other. As we've already seen in other chapters, mastering the art of clear language means clarifying our thoughts and choosing the right words to express them accurately.

The 'curse of knowledge' can cause us to assume that others have the same understanding as us, leading to confusion and misunderstanding. Similarly, when our thoughts are complex or abstract, we may struggle to find the right words to express them. Cultural and language differences can create additional barriers, as our words and their meanings might not translate perfectly across different cultures or languages.

Confidence & Respect

Clarity shows confidence and respect for your audience. People see straight through jargon and unnecessarily complex language in a heartbeat. They often assume that the speaker doesn't know what they're talking about, that they're nervous, or that they're insecure and incompetent. So remember that less is more. Of course, 'clarity' isn't about dumbing it down for your audience; it's about making it easy for them and being your audience's advocate.

In academic and political settings, the tendency is to complicate concepts and make them less accessible. This is often done unconsciously in academia, as this world has developed a standardized style that peers have come to expect from each other. Though it may be tradition to complicate concepts to make them seem more 'academic' or 'professional' or to justify one's research grant, it's useless when you want to reach other humans and create meaningful connections.

Example:

"Improving the efficacy of measurable learning outcomes."

could be expressed as

"improving learning" or "improving learning efficiency," if you want to be specific.

There is no need for the empty, self-indulgent language used in the original version. Remember that clichés and vagueness are usually for people who are either trying to hide the fact that they don't know what they're talking about or have something else to hide. We will look at evasion techniques later in this book, but we will focus on transparency for now.

Exercise

Please read the following text and change it to make it more personal, direct, and interesting. We've provided an example on the next page, but there are many ways to reword this paragraph. (Please note that this is not a real example, and any resemblance to real companies is purely coincidental).

Original text:

"The staff at XYZ Media have been consulting successfully and fostering measurable, tailored solutions for their clients for years. The company's highly experienced media consultants understand and appreciate their clients' requirements to launch and implement cost-effective, cutting-edge solutions strategically and systematically. Their sensitivity to the client's objectives and profound expertise in marketing strategy and social media bring added value and synergy to any project they embark upon."

OK, let's see if we can clean it up ... write your answer on a separate sheet, then check the Sample Answer below.

Sample Answer

"We've been helping our clients profit from advertising and social media for years. Our experienced specialists understand and appreciate your need to increase profits and brand recognition by implementing cost-effective solutions logically and systematically. Our marketing strategy and social media expertise will help you achieve your objectives."

This sample is by no means perfect. Some work still needs to be done, but it's better than the original. The first thing we've done is that we've simplified it. We've cut any words that didn't add to the message. Words like "synergy" have been cut altogether.

The second thing we've done here is we've reworded some of the business jargon to make it more relatable. There is still some jargon left in this text, but we've tried to reduce it to a minimum. The reader or listener is human, regardless of whether they are the cleaner or CEO. Remember this.

The third thing we've done is, instead of speaking in the third person about the company all the time, we've introduced personal pronouns like "we" and personal possessive pronouns like "our" and "your."

Finally, we've tried to be as specific as possible. We've talked about "profits" and "brand recognition" rather than "measurable, tailored solutions." This not only adds to our overall message, but it also adds credibility and makes us more relatable as a business or business professional.

Chapter 4. Powerful Descriptions for Impactful Communication

Speak to create, change, and inspire.
Your words will echo through eternity.

Descriptions can be *creative*, providing memorable images and feelings, or *scientific*, focusing on delivering accurate details. But the true purpose of description is to engage listeners and make the information more memorable, relatable, and interesting.

When you describe something, such as a car engine, you can either give a factual, technical explanation or focus on creating a more subjective, sensory image, emphasizing its power and speed capacity.

You could say:

"The engine is a twin-turbocharged 3.8L V6 with an aluminum block and cylinder heads, pressurized lubrication system, and an intercooled sequential multi-point fuel injection system. It is capable of producing 550 horsepower at 6,400 RPM and 463 lb-ft of torque at 3,200 RPM. This powerplant uses a 24-valve DOHC design, and its force-fed induction comes courtesy of a pair of IHI turbochargers, operating at a maximum boost pressure of 13.5 PSI. Combined with a six-speed dual-clutch transmission, it allows the car to accelerate from 0 to 60 mph in just under 3.5 seconds."

Or you could describe the engine in the following way:

"Picture a snarling beast beneath the hood, its heart throbbing with barely contained ferocity. The engine's roar is a symphony of power, a twin-turbocharged powerhouse of savage speed. Every thundering pulse echoes like a primal drum; each beat resonates raw. The mere whisper of pressure on the pedal and the beast awakens, sending a shiver through its chassis. It's a breathtaking dance of speed and power."

Depending on your audience, both can be appropriate. We will now explore the first type of description, scientific description.

'Scientific' Descriptions

Scientific descriptions are not only used in science and engineering; they are used in every subject. Scientific descriptions are focused on facts. The main objective is to communicate factual information with clarity and precision. It's about clearly explaining the 'what' and 'how' of something. How much detail you provide will always depend on the type of audience.

For example, if you were discussing an autonomous vehicle, you wouldn't be expected to merely describe its shiny exterior or how it feels to drive it. Instead, as we did with our car engine example, you'd need to describe its components and explain how these parts interact to enable self-navigation.

Scientific speaking requires practice. Mastering it improves your speaking skills and refines your thinking process, enabling you to dissect complex subjects into comprehensible units.

The Importance of Scientific Descriptions

The essence of scientific description is its power to clarify a subject so that it leaves no room for misunderstandings. Mastering this technique requires knowing and understanding your subject so well that you can present it to others. It's a test of your comprehension and, therefore, a reflection of your clear thinking. However, while explaining your subject comprehensively is crucial, you should also avoid going into excessive detail. Generally, you should give as much detail as your audience needs- no more, no less.

The primary role of scientific speaking is establishing a bridge of understanding between you and your audience. It's the starting point for further discussions, arguments, and appeals. Clarity, precision, accuracy, logic, truth, and necessity should be your aim when presenting this type of information.

Task: Scientific Descriptions (Example Topic):

Let's look at a simple example to illustrate a scientific description. The diagram illustrates how bees produce honey. Select and report the main features and make comparisons where relevant.

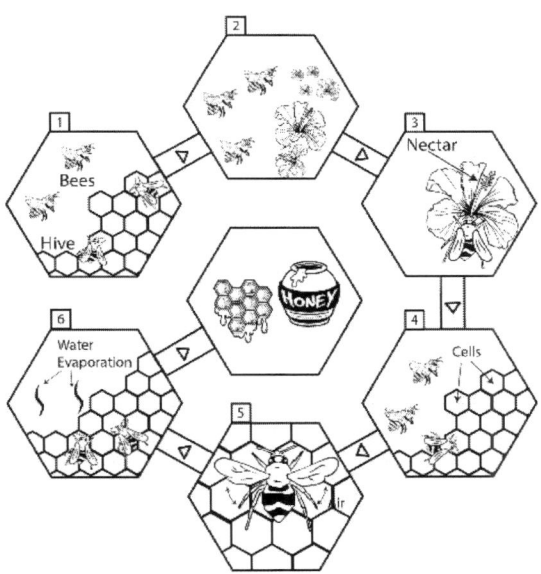

Nectar: A sugary fluid produced by flowers to encourage pollination.
Hive: A dome-shaped or boxlike structure where bees live.
Evaporation: The process of turning from water into vapour.

Basic Process Outline:

Picture 1 – Bees live in a hive

Picture 2 – Bees fly around and visit flowers.

Picture 3 – Bees collect nectar from each flower.

Picture 4 – Nectar is deposited into cells inside the hive.

Picture 5 – Bees flap their wings, which creates air movement.

Picture 6 – Water evaporates from the nectar.

Picture 7 – Honey is left behind.

Plan

It is important to plan the structure of our speaking so that we have included all the elements of the process.

REMEMBER: We must structure our speaking so the listener can understand and learn from what we describe. Imagine the audience can't see the process diagram and needs your help understanding it.

We need an introduction that tells the listener what we are talking about –

Useful Language

COMMON WORD/PHRASE	POSSIBLE ALTERNATIVE PHRASES/SYNONYMS
The diagram	The picture, illustration, image, graphic
illustrates	shows, explains, demonstrates
how	the way in which, the process of
produce	make

- First, we need to give an overview of the whole process without giving specific details.

- We need to plan two sections that **select and report** (describe) the main features of the process.

Exercise 1: Factual Descriptions

Write your description of the process. Follow the Basic Structure outlined below.

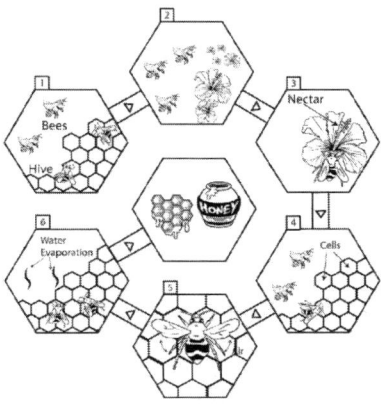

Nectar: A sugary fluid produced by flowers to encourage pollination.
Hive: A dome-shaped or boxlike structure where bees live.
Evaporation: The process of turning from water into vapour.

BASIC STRUCTURE

Section 1	Introduction	Your first sentence.
Section 2	Overview	Describe the whole process in one sentence.
Section 3	Main feature 1	What happens outside the hive?
Section 4	Main feature 2	What happens inside the hive?

Sample Response

The diagram summarizes the process of honey production in beehives.

There are seven key stages in this entire process, beginning with the honey bees building a hive and concluding with the collection and use of the honey.

Firstly, the bees build a dome-shaped or box-like structure, called a hive, in which to live. It consists of many individually built units called cells. Then, the bees leave the hive to search for flowers. They are attracted to flowers by their scent, so they collect nectar, a sticky, sugary substance, from each flower they visit. It is this substance that forms the basis of honey production.

The nectar is deposited into the cells when the bees return to the hive. Next, the nectar is cooled down by the air movement created by the flapping of the bees' wings. This also causes the nectar to lose its water content. Finally, the honey is left as the product of the whole process and can be enjoyed as a deliciously sweet treat.

Exercise 2: Language

Useful Language for Process Descriptions

"The procedure for... is as follows."

"In order to ...the following process takes place."

"First of all,..."

"Then..."

"After that..."

"At the next stage..."

"This is done by..."

"Finally,..."

"This completes the procedure."

Use the useful phrases above to complete the sentences and form a general explanation of a legal process.

_____ a legal case, _____: _____, the plaintiff files the complaint in court. _____, the defendant is served a notice.

_____, the defendant may respond to the complaint. _____, the discovery process occurs. _____, a trial is conducted if a settlement isn't reached. _____, the case resolution procedure.

Answer Key

Remember that while these are the ideal answers according to the phrases provided, minor variations could still be considered correct. The aim is to understand the usage of these phrases in a process description context.

"The procedure for handling a legal case is as follows:

First of all, the complaint is filed in court by the plaintiff.

Then, the defendant is served a notice.

After that, the defendant may respond to the complaint.

In the next stage, the discovery process occurs.

Finally, a trial is conducted if a settlement isn't reached.

This completes the case resolution procedure."

Metaphors & Analogies

Unlock Complex Concepts

The words we use say a lot more than their literal meaning. Highly effective speakers are aware of this. Using suggestive language can stimulate ideas and images that complement your main point. For instance, portraying a colleague as the 'bedrock of our team' implies far more than the words explicitly mean, insinuating their strength, reliability, and foundational role within the group.

What's key is that your descriptions create a clear and vivid picture for your listener.

Consider this: "He is a relentless leader with a sharp eye for detail and a focus on data-driven decisions. He's resilient, always the last to leave the office, a constant example of passion and drive."

Understanding Metaphors and Analogies

Let's talk about metaphors and analogies, two powerful tools used to express ideas through comparison. Though they appear similar, they are used differently.

First, let's consider the metaphor. Picture this: You're telling a friend: "My boss is a shark." You don't mean your boss has fins or lives in the ocean. You mean your boss is aggressive and ready to seize opportunities, just like a shark hunting for prey. The comparison is direct, implying your boss is a shark in behavior. That's a metaphor.

Now, let's move to an analogy. Imagine you're explaining how business communication works.

You might say:

"In any large business, communication can be likened to the nervous system in the human body. Just as the nervous system coordinates and controls all the actions of the body by transmitting signals between different parts, effective business communication ensures smooth functioning by transmitting crucial information between departments and from the business to its customers or clients."

This comparison doesn't mean a business email is the same as a brain signal between two neurons, but it helps the person quickly understand its function by relating it to something they know. This is an analogy.

So, remember this: a metaphor directly states one thing *is* something else to create a vivid picture, while an analogy directly compares, saying something is *like* something else.

Training 1: Distinguishing Between Metaphors and Analogies

Objective: Practice identifying and differentiating between metaphors and analogies.

Instructions:

- Below, you'll find a list of sentences. Some of these contain metaphors, and some contain analogies. Your task is to:

- Identify whether each sentence contains a metaphor or an analogy.

- Explain your reasoning, i.e., why you think it's a metaphor or an analogy.

Hints:

Metaphors often involve a direct comparison, stating one thing is another.

Analogies often explain one thing by likening it to another, showing how they are similar, often in a more elaborate or detailed way.

1. Life is like a box of chocolates; you never know what you're going to get.

2. The classroom was a zoo.

3. Understanding the universe is like unraveling a giant ball of yarn; the more we pull, the more it unravels, revealing complex patterns and layers.

4. Writing a sentence is like building a house; you must lay a strong foundation before building the walls and the roof.

5. Casey Miller's voice is butter to my ears. Could you please find a way to get that audible chocolate on the airwaves?

Answers

1. Analogy

2. Metaphor

3. Analogy

4. Analogy

5. Metaphor

Training 2: Martin Luther King Case Study

Case Study Analysis - "I Have a Dream" by Martin Luther King Jr.

Objective: Identify and analyze the use of metaphors and analogies in Martin Luther King Jr.'s "*I Have a Dream*" speech and discuss how these figures of speech contribute to the effectiveness of his message.

Instructions:

Identification: Carefully read the excerpt from MLK's "*I Have a Dream*" speech. As you review the text, underline or highlight any metaphors and analogies you find.

Analysis: Write down each metaphor or analogy you have identified on a separate paper or document.

For each one:

a. Briefly describe what two things are being compared.

b. Explain the literal meaning of the metaphor or analogy.

c. Explain the symbolic or implied meaning of the metaphor or analogy.

Reflection: Reflect on the effectiveness of these metaphors and analogies. Discuss the following questions:

a. How do these metaphors and analogies contribute to the overall message of the speech?

b. How do they help simplify complex ideas, making the speech more accessible to a wide audience?

c. How do they add emotional weight and rhetorical power to King's message?

Presentation: Prepare a brief presentation summarizing your findings. Please include examples of the identified metaphors and analogies, your analysis of their meanings, and your thoughts on their effectiveness.

Discussion: If you are an instructor or teacher, you can open the floor for a class discussion after the presentations. Discuss any differing interpretations of the metaphors and analogies and their impact on the overall message of the speech.

Remember, the aim of this exercise is not just to identify the use of metaphors and analogies but also to understand their crucial role in making a message more impactful and relatable. As you engage with this exercise, consider how using these figures of speech could enhance your public speaking and communication skills.

Here is part of the legendary "*I Have a Dream*" speech by Martin Luther King Jr. on the 28th of August, 1963, at the Lincoln Memorial, Washington D.C.:

"I am not unmindful that some of you have come here out of great trials and tribulations. Some of you have come fresh from narrow jail cells. Some of you have come from areas where your quest for freedom left you battered by the storms of persecution and staggered by the winds of police brutality. You have been the veterans of creative suffering. Continue to work with the faith that unearned suffering is redemptive.

Go back to Mississippi, go back to Alabama, go back to South Carolina, go back to Georgia, go back to Louisiana, go back to the slums and ghettos of our northern cities, knowing that somehow this situation can and will be changed. Let us not wallow in the valley of despair.

I say to you today, my friends, so even though we face the difficulties of today and tomorrow, I still have a dream. It is a dream deeply rooted in the American dream.

I have a dream that one day, this nation will rise up and live out the true meaning of its creed: "We hold these truths to be self-evident: that all men are created equal."

I have a dream that one day, on the red hills of Georgia, the sons of former slaves and the sons of former slaveowners will be able to sit down together at the table of brotherhood.

I have a dream that one day, even the state of Mississippi, a state sweltering with the heat of injustice, sweltering with the heat of oppression, will be transformed into an oasis of freedom and justice.

I have a dream that my four little children will one day live in a nation where they will not be judged by the color of their skin but by the content of their character.

I have a dream today.

I have a dream that one day, down in Alabama, with its vicious racists, with its governor having his lips dripping with the words of interposition and nullification; one day right there in Alabama, little black boys and black girls will be able to join hands with little white boys and white girls as sisters and brothers.

I have a dream today.

I have a dream that one day, every valley shall be exalted, every hill and mountain shall be made low, the rough places will be made plain, and the crooked places will be made straight, and the glory of the Lord shall be revealed, and all flesh shall see it together.

This is our hope. This is the faith that I go back to the South with. With this faith, we will be able to hew out of the mountain of despair a stone of hope. With this faith, we will be able to transform the jangling discords of our nation into a beautiful symphony of brotherhood. With this faith, we will be able to work together, to pray together, to struggle together, to go to jail together, to stand up for freedom together, knowing that we will be free one day.

This will be the day when all of God's children will be able to sing with a new meaning, "My country, 'tis of thee, sweet land of liberty, of thee I sing. Land where my fathers died, land of the pilgrims' pride, from every mountainside, let freedom ring."

And if America is to be a great nation, this must become true. So let freedom ring from the prodigious hilltops of New Hampshire. Let freedom ring from the mighty mountains of New York. Let freedom ring from the heightening Alleghenies of Pennsylvania!

Let freedom ring from the snowcapped Rockies of Colorado!

Let freedom ring from the curvaceous slopes of California!

But not only that, let freedom ring from Stone Mountain of Georgia!

Let freedom ring from Lookout Mountain of Tennessee!

Let freedom ring from every hill and molehill of Mississippi. From every mountainside, let freedom ring.

And when this happens, when we allow freedom to ring, when we let it ring from every village and every hamlet, from every state and every city, we will be able to speed up that day when all of God's children, black men and white men, Jews, and Gentiles, Protestants, and Catholics, will be able to join hands and sing in the words of the old Negro spiritual, "Free at last! free at last! thank God Almighty, we are free at last! "

Sample Responses:

Identification: Some examples of metaphors and analogies in the excerpt include: "battered by the storms of persecution," "sweltering with the heat of injustice," "transform the jangling discords of our nation into a beautiful symphony of brotherhood," "hew out of the mountain of despair a stone of hope," "let freedom ring," etc.

Analysis:

a. For the metaphor "battered by the storms of persecution," the two things being compared are the hardships faced by African Americans and a destructive storm.

b. Literally, the phrase suggests someone being physically battered by a storm.

c. Symbolically, it represents the brutal hardships and persecutions the African American community faced during the Civil Rights Movement.

Reflection:

a. The metaphors and analogies significantly contribute to the overall message of the speech by painting vivid pictures of the African-American community's struggles, hopes, and dreams. They make the abstract concepts of injustice, freedom, and hope tangible and relatable.

b. By using metaphors and analogies, King could simplify complex social issues and make them accessible to a wide audience. People from different backgrounds could understand and connect with the speech.

c. The metaphors and analogies add emotional weight and rhetorical power to King's message. They evoke strong emotions, inspiring people to act and effect change.

Create Memorable Impressions

Metaphors and analogies not only simplify complexity but also make ideas more memorable. They create vivid mental images, enabling our brains to grasp and retain information.

For example, when explaining the importance of diversified investments, comparing it to the expression 'not putting all your eggs in one basket' immediately simplifies and makes it visual. The image it creates reinforces the concept of diversification, making it more memorable.

Using analogies and metaphors can greatly enhance the impact of your communication, leaving a lasting impression. They should also be simple to grasp for your audience yet vivid enough to leave a lasting impression. However, be careful not to overuse them, which can confuse or dilute your main message. As with all communication techniques, it's about balance and relevance to the topic at hand.

Here are some examples:

Navigating the Career Labyrinth: If you are talking about a person's career journey, you could use a labyrinth or maze as a metaphor.

"Navigating your career is like finding your way through a labyrinth. It may involve unexpected turns and dead ends, but with patience and perseverance, you will eventually find your way to the center - your ultimate career goal."

Iceberg of Knowledge: When discussing the breadth and depth of one's expertise or knowledge, you might use an iceberg metaphor.

"Your current knowledge is just the tip of the iceberg. Under the water's surface lies a vast expanse of information and expertise you have yet to discover."

Garden of Innovation: A garden can be an effective metaphor for discussing innovation or creative thinking.

"Innovation isn't a lightning bolt of an idea that strikes randomly. It's more like a garden. It needs time, care, and patience. Ideas, like seeds, need to be nurtured and fed. Only then will they grow and flourish."

Bridge of Collaboration: When illustrating the idea of teamwork and collaboration, you can compare it to building a bridge.

"Working as a team is like building a bridge. Each piece, no matter how small, plays a crucial role in the strength and stability of the structure. We can span vast and challenging obstacles when all pieces work together."

Fitness Training for the Mind: You can compare constant learning and personal development with physical fitness training.

"Keeping your mind sharp and expanding your knowledge is like training for a marathon. Consistent effort and discipline build mental fitness and stamina, helping you tackle intellectual challenges more effectively."

Be Mindful of Context

While the power of metaphors and analogies is immense, it's important to use them wisely. Ensure they are relevant to your audience and resonate with their experiences or cultural contexts. Also, be mindful of not oversimplifying or distorting the original concept.

The most impactful metaphors and analogies resonate with the listener's experiences and emotions.

So, for example, if you are talking to an electrical engineer, instead of saying,

"Working as a team is like building a bridge,...."

you might say;

"Working as a team is a lot like the functioning of an electrical circuit. Each component, whether it's a resistor, a capacitor, or a transistor, has a specific role to play in the overall operation of the system. When all components are properly connected and working together, the circuit functions smoothly, and electricity flows efficiently, powering up the whole system. Similarly, in a team, when each member performs their role efficiently and collaboratively, the team functions optimally, driving the project or organization towards its goals."

Remember, the goal is not to dilute the complexity but to unlock it, making it understandable, relatable, and memorable. Metaphors and analogies are powerful keys to achieving this, adding clarity and color to your communication.

So, next time you're faced with explaining a complex idea, remember to paint a picture and tell a story - use a metaphor or analogy. It might be the bridge your audience needs to understand and remember your point.

Training 3: Metaphors

Objective: To improve understanding and creation of metaphors for enhancing communication.

Activity Description:

Below, you will find sentences with missing words. Each sentence should form a metaphor when completed. Fill in the gaps to create a metaphor, ensuring it is logical, creative, and engaging.

Instructions:

1. Read each sentence carefully and understand the context.
2. Fill in the blank to complete the metaphor. Try to use words that create a vivid and memorable image.
3. Please write down your answers and review them. Are the metaphors clear? Are they creative and engaging? Would they be memorable to someone who heard them?
4. Try to use your metaphors in real-life conversations or written communications and observe the reactions of your listeners or readers.

Through this activity, you will practice creating your own metaphors and improve your ability to use metaphors effectively in communication.

"Working on this project is like climbing a _____. Every step brings a new challenge, but the view from the top makes the effort worthwhile."

"Building a successful career is like growing a _____. It needs regular attention, care, and patience to bloom fully."

"Our minds are like _____; they can expand with knowledge, just as a sponge absorbs water."

"Innovation in our company is the _____ that fuels our growth and drives us forward."

"Learning a new language opens up a new _____; it gives us a fresh perspective and helps us understand different cultures."

"Working as a team is like building a _____. No matter how small their role, each member contributes to the strength and stability of the entire structure."

Suggested Answers:

"Working on this project is like climbing a mountain/rock wall/tall tree. Every step brings a new challenge, but the view from the top makes the effort worthwhile."

"Building a successful career is like growing a tree/garden/flower. It needs regular attention, care, and patience to bloom fully."

"Our minds are like sponges/libraries/vessels; they can expand with knowledge, just as a sponge absorbs water."

"Innovation in our company is the engine/fuel/heartbeat that fuels our growth and drives us forward."

"Learning a new language opens up a new world/window/universe; it gives us a fresh perspective and helps us understand different cultures."

"Working as a team is like building a bridge/dam/house. No matter how small their role, each member contributes to the strength and stability of the entire structure."

As long as the chosen word fits the context and conveys the meaning effectively, it can be considered a correct answer.

Training 4: Analogies

Objective: Improve your ability to use analogies effectively.

Instructions:

1. Read both the metaphor and the analogy carefully.
2. Consider which of the two resonates more with you or which you believe communicates the concept of "Change Management" more effectively.
3. Please write down your preferred option and explain why you chose it. Consider its clarity, vividness, relevance to the topic, and how memorable it is.

   There is no right or wrong answer here. Please note that metaphors and analogies often overlap. The following examples could also be considered metaphorical.

Changing Seasons

"Managing change in our organization is like the changing seasons. Just as each season gradually gives way to the next, bringing new weather, flora, and fauna, our organization must adapt to different stages of our business cycle. We must shed old ways like autumn leaves and embrace the fresh buds of innovative practices."

Steering a Ship

"Steering through change is like being the captain of a large ship. As a captain, you must constantly monitor the winds, the tides, and the condition of your ship. It's about adjusting the sails, navigating around storms, and ensuring the crew is prepared and motivated to face the voyage ahead. In the same way, managing change requires constant vigilance, flexibility, and the ability to motivate your team."

Follow-up Activity

Once you have some notes, write your own metaphor for change management. If you are working with a partner, you can compare your answers when you have finished.

Training 5: Mastering Metaphors & Analogies

Objective: This exercise will allow you to practice creating metaphors and analogies. Remember, the goal is to vividly convey meaning or simplify complex ideas.

Part 1: Metaphors

Choose any five items from the list below and create your own unique metaphors:

1. A book

2. The ocean

3. A storm

4. A mountain

5. A long line at the bank

6. A packed subway train

7. A deserted city street at night

    Example: "A book is a window to another world."

Part 2: Analogies

Choose five items from the list below and create an analogy for each. Try to simplify or clarify a complex idea.

1. The Internet

2. A mobile phone

3. A crowded marketplace

4. A satellite orbiting the earth

5. A busy restaurant kitchen

6. A computer algorithm

7. An airport during holiday season

Example: "The internet is like a giant library. Just as a library houses countless books with a multitude of information, the internet hosts a vast array of websites and data from around the world."

Remember, creativity is key. Challenge yourself to think outside the box and use vivid, unique comparisons to craft your metaphors and analogies.

Chapter 5. Repetition

Speak it once, it's heard; repeat it, it's believed.

Repetition is a powerful speaking tool. It can emphasize key points, make your speech memorable, and reinforce your core message.

Here's how to use it effectively:

Identify Your Key Points:

Decide the important points or concepts you want your audience to remember. This could be your main message, a policy proposal, or a key fact. Once identified, these will be the elements you'll aim to repeat and reiterate throughout your speech.

Change the language:

When using repetition, it's not only about saying the same sentences repeatedly. It's about conveying the same idea or key points in different ways, using different words or perspectives. It creates consistency in your message.

Anaphora

Anaphora is when you repeat a word or phrase at the start of consecutive clauses or sentences.

An example is Martin Luther King Jr.'s famous "I Have a Dream" speech, where *"I Have a Dream"* is repeated at the start of multiple sentences.

Multiple Choice

Choose which of the following examples does not use the technique of anaphora:

"It's a bright, beautiful day. It's a perfect time for a walk. It's a great time to be alive."

"Mary looked at the stars. She thought about the vastness of the universe."

"We shall fight on the beaches. We shall fight on the landing grounds. We shall fight in the fields and in the streets."

"He loved the smell of old books. He loved the quiet of the library. He loved the world of stories."

Answer Key:

Yes (Repetition of "It's a" at the beginning of each sentence)

No (No repetition at the beginning of the sentences)

Yes (Repetition of "We shall fight" at the beginning of each sentence)

Yes (Repetition of "He loved" at the beginning of each sentence)

Practice

1. Write a paragraph about the beauty of nature using anaphora.
2. Use anaphora in a paragraph about the importance of learning.
3. Create a short piece about the excitement of travel using anaphora.

   Please note that with this type of exercise, there isn't necessarily a single correct answer because the students will create original pieces.

Epiphora

Epiphora/Epistrophe: Repeating a word or phrase at the end of successive clauses.

An example of this is the famous Winston Churchill speech, where he emphasizes:

"We shall fight on the beaches, we shall fight on the landing grounds, we shall fight in the fields and in the streets, we shall fight in the hills."

The effect of this is powerful.

Another example comes from Abraham Lincoln's Gettysburg Address:

"that this nation, under God, shall have a new birth of freedom—and that government of the people,

by the people,

for the people,

shall not perish from the earth."

This rhetorical device can effectively emphasize key themes and create a lasting impression on listeners or readers.

Fill in the Blanks with Epiphora

Fill in the blanks with the same word or phrase to create epiphora. The word or phrase should fit the context of each sentence.

"In our company, we value .... in our products, ... in our processes, and .... in our mindset."

"We stand for .... in our homes, ... in our communities, ... in our nation."

"We must cherish the .... for its beauty, protect the .... for its biodiversity, and respect the .... for its resources."

Suggested Answers

"In our company, we value innovation in our products, innovation in our processes, and innovation in our mindset."

"We stand for justice in our homes, justice in our communities, justice in our nation."

"We must cherish the earth for its beauty, protect the earth for its biodiversity, and respect the earth for its resources."

The above are only suggested answers. Your answer is correct if you have added a different word that makes sense.

Mesodiplosis

Mesodiplosis: Repetition of a word or phrase in the middle of successive clauses or sentences.

"We are troubled on every side, yet <u>not</u> distressed; we are perplexed, but <u>not</u> in despair; persecuted, but <u>not</u> forsaken; cast down, but <u>not</u> destroyed..."

(Second Epistle to the Corinthians)

Underline

In the following example, underline the word(s) that make the mesodiplosis.

"One, but not two; three, but not four; five, but not six."

Answer

"One, <u>but not</u> two; three, <u>but not</u> four; five, <u>but not</u> six."

Anadiplosis

Anadiplosis is when you repeat the last word or phrase from one sentence or clause at the beginning of the next. This can help create a sense of continuity and connection between your points.

"He started <u>a business</u>, <u>a business</u> that ruined him financially."

Crafting Sentences with Anadiplosis in a Professional Context

Write a sentence or two for each of the following prompts, practicing the use of Anadiplosis. Your aim is to repeat the last word or phrase from one sentence or clause at the beginning of the next sentence or clause.

Examples:

Prompt: Describe the sense of achievement a team feels after completing a challenging project.

Anadiplosis: The team completed the project, a project that had tested their skills and resolve.

Prompt: Discuss the impact of a new policy introduced in the workplace.

Anadiplosis: The new policy was introduced, a policy that led to significant improvements in efficiency.

Prompt: Write about the process of strategically planning for a company's growth.

Anadiplosis: He was involved in strategic planning, planning that would steer the company towards greater growth.

Prompt: Capture the anticipation before the launch of a new product.

Anadiplosis: The product launch was imminent, a launch that had the potential to redefine the market.

Keep It Engaging:

Repetition is about emphasizing and underscoring your main points. Ensure your speech maintains variety and your repeated points are not dull but instead highlighted through your creative use of language.

Pair Repetition with Other Techniques:

While repetition can be very effective on its own, pairing it with other communication techniques, such as storytelling, the use of data, or emotional appeals, can make it even more powerful.

Remember, the goal of repetition in speaking is to make your message clear, memorable, and persuasive. It's about helping your audience understand your points and engraining your key message in their minds.

Alliteration

Alliteration: Using the same consonant sound at the beginning of each stressed syllable in a line or passage can make a phrase catchier.

In the U.S. presidential race of 2000, American voters had to choose between George W. Bush's "compassionate conservatism." And Al Gore's "prosperity and progress."

Decades before, Martin Luther King Jr. hoped that black Americans would " not be judged by the color of their skin but by the content of their character."

Other examples are:

"Build better business bonds by being a bridge, not a barrier."

"Cultivating a culture of continuous improvement creates confident companies."

"Profitability is possible with proper planning, perseverance, and patience."

Practice

Think of your own alliteration. Write your phrase or sentence in your notebook.

Chapter 6. Speaking Well: Language & Pronunciation for Effective Workplace Conversations

Eloquence is expressing truth in a way that your listener clearly understands.

A lack of vocabulary can sometimes limit our ability to express our thoughts accurately. Sometimes, while speaking, we can find ourselves stumbling over our words, trying to find the right grammar and phrasing to express our thoughts accurately. Even if we know the words and we've used them a thousand times before, this can still happen. We've all been there - mid-sentence, suddenly unsure of how to continue or questioning our choice of words. It's a common struggle, an inevitable part of the speaking journey.

But what if you can turn this struggle into a strength?

The Power of Words

From Plato to Gandhi, Roosevelt, Churchill, Mandela, Martin Luther King, to the likes of Tupac Shakur or Steve Jobs—the reason they live in our memories is their words. People who can speak eloquently are perceived differently. They are considered more intelligent, more aware, and thus treated differently.

At work, positive language can dramatically impact interactions. For instance, think about the effect these two responses might have on the person who hears them:

"I will have that information for you by 2 p.m."

VS.

"I can't get that to you until 2 p.m."

They both mean the same thing but express very different messages.

Which one do you think gives a better impression of the speaker?

In this case, positive phrasing doesn't just communicate the same factual information—it conveys an attitude of proactivity, reliability, and commitment. It's a subtle but powerful way to improve your professional interactions and leave a more positive impression.

Compare the following scenarios:

Providing updates on a project:

"The project is progressing well; we've already completed three milestones."

VS.

"We're not done yet. There are still several parts left."

Handling a delay:

"We are working diligently to finish the process and deliver results as soon as possible."

VS.

"We're running late, and it will take longer."

Responding to feedback or criticism:

"I appreciate your feedback and will incorporate it into my future work."

VS.

"That's the way I do things."

Expressing disagreement:

"I see where you're coming from, but might I suggest an alternative perspective?"

VS.

"I disagree!"

These differences can significantly influence the perception and impression others form about the speaker.

Training 1: Positive vs. Negative Language

Below are several work-related scenarios. For each situation, one response is provided. Decide whether the response is positive or negative. Rewrite the negative statements using positive language.

Example:

Scenario 1: A customer is complaining about a delayed order.

Response: "I'm very sorry for the delay. I have checked with our warehouse. But unfortunately, your order cannot be delivered until next week. I cannot check the exact delivery date because our system does not allow it."

This response uses negative language that can negatively impact the customer's perception. We can rephrase it: "I'm very sorry for the delay. I have checked with our warehouse, and your order will be ready for delivery by next week. I can give you an estimated delivery date." Much better!

Now it's your turn:

Scenario 2: You're giving feedback on a colleague's presentation.

"The presentation lacked crucial data."

How can you say this better?

Scenario 3: A coworker asks you to help with a task, but you're already busy with your own tasks.

"I can't help you; I have too much of my own work to do."

How can you say this better?

Scenario 4: Your team member made a mistake.

"You shouldn't have done it this way."

How can you say this better?

Scenario 5: A team member hasn't met their performance targets for the quarter.

"Your performance this quarter hasn't met our expectations."

How can you say this better?

Scenario 6: You are informing your team about a change in company policy.

"The company is no longer allowing remote work on Fridays."

How can you say this better?

Scenario 7: A colleague asks you for a meeting when you're already fully booked.

"Today's schedule is packed. Could we find a time early next week to meet?"

How can you say this better?

Review each of your responses and think about how it impacts the listener's perception.

Suggested Answers:

Scenario 2: You're giving feedback on a colleague's presentation.

"Including more data could make your presentation even more compelling."

Scenario 3: A coworker asks you to help with a task, but you're already busy with your own tasks.

"Once I finish my current task, I'll be delighted to help you."

Scenario 4: Your team member made a mistake.

"Let's explore how we can avoid this issue in the future."

Scenario 5: A team member hasn't met their performance targets for the quarter.

"Let's discuss how we can strategize and provide support for improving your performance in the next quarter."

Scenario 6: You are informing your team about a change in company policy.

"The company has updated its policy to include dedicated in-office collaboration time every Friday."

Scenario 7: A colleague asks you for a meeting when you're already fully booked.

"Today's schedule is packed. Could we find a time early next week to meet?" This is already positive.

Using Language for Effect

Bill Gates is regarded as clear, persuasive, insightful, and brilliant. But he uses basic language. He's not a natural public speaker, but he offers insights. He focuses on telling simple, clear stories that he is passionate about.

Becoming articulate is not a straightforward journey. We constantly need to test, tweak, and be mindful of context. It's normal to encounter problems when experimenting with words we've heard or read. The aim here is to embody professionalism and intelligence without sounding like you are trying to manipulate your audience's opinion of you.

So, what do the most skilled speakers and writers do?

- The most skillful communicators focus on meaning over style.

- Their style and words are only there to help their main message.

- They use language to help people understand ideas and concepts.

- They don't use words that distract unless they mean to distract.

- They don't use words to feed their ego.

- They can be professional without resorting to obscure or unnatural language.

Beautiful Language

Although we may not see everyday language as beautiful, it can be. There are small changes you can make to improve your speaking quickly, and the best thing is that it has a subliminal effect, so most people won't consciously notice the change.

For this section, beauty is the emotion stirred by words and the imagery they create. It could be as simple as the crunch of autumn leaves under your shoes, the smell of a summer morning, or the warm glow of a vibrant sunset. Everyday language can be beautiful when used strategically. A stroke of beauty can enhance even the most straightforward communication, such as a business proposal, making the message more impactful and interesting.

Swapping "with" for "of" to create a more vivid description:

Before: "They constructed a raft with driftwood and old ropes."

After: "They constructed a raft of driftwood and old ropes."

Leaving out "is" to infuse a sense of gravity or seriousness:

Before: "Do you think it is wise to sell all our assets now?"

After: "Do you think it is wise to sell all our assets now?"

Leave out the second "is" to improve rhythm.

Before: "Every project is a challenge; every obstacle is an opportunity."

After: "Every project is a challenge, every obstacle is an opportunity."

Employing "her" instead of "that she was" for a concise yet impactful statement:

Before: "I found that she was sharp and witty."

After: "I found her sharp and witty."

Using a comma in place of "are" to infuse drama:

Before: "These are the children who dared to dream."

After: "These, the children who dared to dream."

Omitting "that is" to streamline a sentence:

Before: "I have a passion for everything that is language-related."

After: "I have a passion for everything ~~that is~~ language-related."

Replacing "-ful" with "a source of" to enrich an expression:

Before: "His intermittent attendance is disruptive for them all."

After: "His intermittent attendance is a source of disruption for them all."

Please note that this change makes the sentence longer, so it's important to use it only to add variety to your communication rather than continuously relying on it.

Exchanging "about" for "of" can make a sentence sound better, as exemplified by:

Before: "There's speculation about a product launch, but the marketing lead knows nothing about the tech segment."

After: "There's speculation of a product launch, but the marketing lead knows nothing of the tech segment."

Substituting "very" with the superlative"-est of" to add emphasis:

Before: "It's a very bright morning."

After: "It's the brightest of mornings."

Training 2: Simple Eloquence

As mentioned earlier, the key to clear speaking is simplicity. Redundant expressions, filler words, overly complex jargon, and complex sentence structures are usually unnecessary.

This doesn't mean dumbing down your language or ideas but presenting them in the most straightforward way possible. Keeping your language simple allows your message to shine through, making it easier for your audience to understand and remember.

Instructions: Rewrite the following sentences to eliminate any unnecessary language. Then, check your answers on the next page.

Before: "I'm studying hard in order to pass the exam."

After: "I'm studying hard ~~in order~~ to pass the exam."

Before: "Despite the fact that it was raining, we decided to go for a walk."

Before: "She was happy due to the fact that her team won."

Before: "He is able to swim very fast."

Before: "In spite of the fact that he was tired, he kept working."

Before: "She has the ability to solve complex problems."

Before: "I don't know whether or not I should go to the party."

Before: "In spite of the difficulties, we must proceed."

Before: "I came to a realization that I was wrong."

Before: "We should give consideration to all the options."

Answers

Replacing "in order to" with "to" for succinctness:

After: "I'm studying hard to pass the exam."

Dropping "the fact that" for more directness:

After: "Despite it raining, we decided to go for a walk."

Replacing "due to the fact that" with "because" for simplicity:

After: "She was happy because her team won."

Substituting "is able to" with "can" to make a sentence less wordy:

After: "He can swim very fast."

Replacing "in spite of the fact that" with "although" to streamline:

After: "Although he was tired, he kept working."

Replacing "has the ability to" with "can" for brevity:

After: "She can solve complex problems."

Replacing "whether or not" with "whether" to simplify:

After: "I don't know whether I should go to the party."

Using "despite" instead of "in spite of" for conciseness:

After: "Despite the difficulties, we must proceed."

Replacing "came to a realization" with "realized" to streamline:

After: "I realized I was wrong."

Substituting "give consideration to" with "consider" for brevity:

After: "We should consider all the options."

Common Errors

English grammar can often be overwhelming, with so many rules and exceptions. But grammar, in essence, is the roadmap of language. It guides us in structuring sentences, ensuring our ideas flow logically and clearly. Understand the logic behind these rules and practice them regularly. Your sentences become more coherent and powerful as you become comfortable with grammar.

While the principles of grammar apply broadly to both writing and speaking, some issues are more commonly problematic in spoken English, even for native speakers. Here are some examples:

"You and I" vs. "You and me": This issue is commonly heard in casual conversation. Even though the rule is the same as in writing, people often use "you and me" as the subject of a sentence when it should be "you and I."

People sometimes do this consciously to signal different levels of formality. For example, "you and me" with friends "you and I" in formal settings.

Double negatives: In some English dialects, double negatives are used for emphasis. However, in standard English, a double negative creates a positive statement.

Avoid using double negatives in your sentences.

Imagine Mary saying;

"We don't have no eggs left, because I haven't had no time to go to the shop."

Most people easily understand this sentence, but it doesn't leave a great impression of Mary and her linguistic competence. Mary might be highly educated, extremely intelligent, and competent, but shouting "We don't have no eggs left, because I haven't had no time to go to the shop," doesn't help her.

However, if Mary instead says;

"We don't have any eggs left, because I've had no time to go to the shop…"

her friend will instantly grasp the dire egg crisis, and Mary will preserve her impeccable reputation.

"Can I" vs. "May I": Traditionally, "can" refers to ability, and "may" refers to permission.

However, in informal speech, many people use "can I" when asking permission.

Traditional usage:

"Can I lift this heavy rock?" In 'traditional English,' this question is asking about ability. Is the person physically able to lift the heavy rock?

"May I use your laptop?" This question is asking for permission. Is the person allowed to use the other person's laptop?

Informal speech:

"Can I use your pen?" In this case, "Can I" is used to ask for permission in an informal setting. Although traditionally "may" would be used, it's common to hear "can" in this context.

"Was" vs. "Were" in the subjunctive: The subjunctive mood is used to discuss hypothetical or non-real situations.

Even though the correct form is "were" (as in "If I were rich, I would buy a helicopter"), many people use "was" in informal conversation ("If I was rich, I would buy a football club").

Incorrect verb tense: People often use simpler tenses instead of correct ones in casual conversation.

For example, you might hear "I seen it" instead of "I have seen it" or "I saw it."

"Who" vs. "Whom": Like in writing, this issue frequently comes up in speech, and most people default to using "who" in all situations.

In practice, most people use "who" in both cases in informal speech because "whom" can sound overly formal or archaic. However, in more formal contexts, especially in writing, use "who" and "whom" correctly.

A quick trick to determine whether to use "who" or "whom" is to answer your question with a pronoun.

Who: When asking questions, if the answer uses "he," "she," "they," or "I," then "who" is correct.

Whom: If the answer uses "him," "her," "them," or "me," then "whom" is correct.

For example:

Question: "Who/Whom did you see?"

Answer: "I saw him."

Therefore, "Whom did you see?" is correct.

Question: "Who/Whom is calling?"

Answer: "He is calling."

Therefore, "Who is calling?" is correct.

The same rule applies to questions, statements, and clauses.

"Who" is used as a subject to refer to the person doing the action, while "whom" is used as an object to refer to the person receiving the action.

Consider these examples:

Statement with "who": "This is the artist who painted this masterpiece."

The artist is the one doing the action of painting, so "who" is appropriate.

Statement with "whom": "This is the boy whom the dog followed."

In this sentence, the boy is receiving the action (being followed by the dog), so "whom" is appropriate.

But remember, in informal speech, it's commonly acceptable to use "who" in both cases.

So you might often hear, "This is the boy who the dog followed."

While this might make grammar purists cringe, it's widely accepted in everyday conversation.

Note: You can also say, "This is the boy ~~whom~~ the dog followed."

Just be mindful when you're in a more formal context or when your communication needs to be polished—this is when the "who" vs. "whom" distinction matters.

Pronunciation Mistakes

Pronunciation can be challenging in English because, often, the spelling of a word doesn't correspond directly to how it's pronounced. Even native speakers sometimes pronounce words incorrectly.

Here are some examples of commonly mispronounced words:

Edinburgh: /ˈɛdɪnbərə/ or /ˈɛdɪnbrə/, not /ˈɛdɪnbɜːɡ/. The pronunciation of "Edinburgh" often confuses non-British English speakers because it doesn't seem to follow conventional pronunciation rules based on its spelling.

In English, "Edinburgh" is pronounced as "Edin-bur-uh," or "Edin-bruh," not "Edin-burg."

Here is a breakdown:

"Edin" sounds like "Edin" in Edwin, where the "e" sounds like the "e" in "bed," and "din" sounds like "din" in "dinner."

The "-burgh" part is where people often get confused. Despite the "-burgh" ending, it's not pronounced like "burg" in "hamburger." Instead, it sounds like "bur-uh" or "bruh"– with the "uh" being very soft, almost silent.

So, together, you get "Edin-bur-uh" or "Edin-bruh."

Many other place names in the UK have similar pronunciation rules, especially those ending in "-borough" or "-burgh."

Espresso: /ɛˈsprɛsoʊ/, not /ɛkˈsprɛsoʊ/. This word is often pronounced as "eXpresso" when it should be pronounced as "espresso."

Athlete: /ˈæθˌliːt/, not /æθˈiːˌlit/. Some people mistakenly add an extra syllable, pronouncing it as "ath-e-lete." The correct pronunciation is "ath-lete."

Nuclear: /ˈnuːkliər/, not /ˌnjuːkʊˈlɪər/

This is often mispronounced as "nu-cu-lar." The correct pronunciation is "nu-clear."

Library: /ˈlaɪbreri/, not /ˈlaɪberi/

Some people leave out the first "r" and pronounce it as "li-bary." The correct pronunciation is "li-brary."

Often: /ˈɔːf(ə)n/ and /ˈɔːftən/ -- Correct. Both are acceptable pronunciations.

The debate over pronouncing the "t" in "often" is longstanding.

Traditionally, the "t" was silent, like in "soften," but the pronunciation with the "t" sound has become very common and is now also considered correct in standard English.

Jewelry: /ˈdʒuːəlri/, not /ˈdʒuːləri/ or /dʒuːˈɛləri/

The correct pronunciation is "jewl-ry," but many people mispronounce it as "jew-lery" or "jew-el-er-y."

Mischievous: /ˈmɪstʃɪvəs/, not /ˌmɪsˈtʃiːviːəs/

Often mispronounced as "miss-chee-vee-us," the correct pronunciation is "miss-chiv-us."

Pronunciation: /prəˌnʌnsiˈeɪʃən/, not /proʊˌnaʊnˈsiːˈeɪʃən/

Ironically, the word 'pronunciation' is often mispronounced. It's not "pro-noun-ciation," but "pro-nun-ciation."

Quinoa: /ˈkiːnwɑː/, not /ˈkwɪnoʊə/

Despite appearances, this grain's name is pronounced "keen-wah" in English, not "quin-oa."

Raspberry: /ˈræzˌbɛri/, not /ˈræspˌbɛri/

The "p" in "raspberry" is silent, so it is correctly pronounced as "raz-ber-ee," not "rasp-berry."

Worcestershire: /ˈwʊstərʃɪr/ or /ˈwʊstərʃər/, not /wɔːrsɛstərʃaɪr/

This British place name and sauce is a real tongue twister for non-British speakers, even native ones. It is pronounced "woo-ster-sheer," or "woo-ster-shuh," not as it is spelled.

Remember, pronunciation can also vary based on regional accents and dialects, so there may be more than one "correct" way to pronounce a word, depending on where you are. Spoken language is often more flexible than written language. However, you'll want to aim for standard English for formal or professional speaking situations.

How to Pronounce Words

What is the International Phonetic Alphabet (IPA)?

Imagine you're trying to describe a color to someone. It would be really difficult without just showing them the color. The IPA is a tool that does the same for sounds. Instead of trying to describe how a sound is made, we can show an IPA symbol.

Why do we need it?

English spelling can be tricky. Words like "though" and "through" look similar but sound different. Conversely, "two" and "too" sound the same but look different. The IPA helps to clear up this confusion by giving each sound its unique symbol.

How do you use it?

Look at the symbol: Each symbol in the IPA chart represents a specific sound.

Say the sound: Try to produce the sound that the symbol represents. The symbol will always stand for the same sound, no matter which word it's in.

Match sounds to spelling: When you see an IPA transcription of a word, like /kæt/ for "cat," it shows you how to pronounce the word by breaking it down sound by sound.

Please note that this chart is a simplified version of the International Phonetic Alphabet (IPA) chart for English. The IPA is a system where each symbol is associated with a particular English sound.

International Phonetic Alphabet (IPA)

Consonants:

p as in pin: /p/

b as in bin: /b/

t as in two: /t/

d as in do: /d/

k as in key: /k/

g as in go: /g/

ʧ as in chin: /ʧ/

ʤ as in gin: /ʤ/

f as in fan: /f/

v as in van: /v/

θ as in thin: /θ/

ð as in this: /ð/

s as in so: /s/

z as in zoo: /z/

ʃ as in she: /ʃ/

ʒ as in vision: /ʒ/

h as in hi: /h/

m as in me: /m/

n as in no: /n/

ŋ as in song: /ŋ/

l as in love: /l/

r as in red: /r/

j as in yes: /j/

w as in we: /w/

Vowels:

iː as in see: /iː/

ɪ as in sit: /ɪ/

e as in bed: /e/

æ as in cat: /æ/

ɑː as in car: /ɑː/

ɔː as in saw: /ɔː/

ʊ as in book: /ʊ/

uː as in shoe: /uː/

ʌ as in but: /ʌ/

ɜː as in bird: /ɜː/

eɪ as in say: /eɪ/

aɪ as in five: /aɪ/

ɔɪ as in boy: /ɔɪ/

aʊ as in now: /aʊ/

oʊ as in go: /oʊ/

ɪə as in here: /ɪə/

eə as in hair: /eə/

ʊə as in sure: /ʊə/

Chapter 7. Answer Difficult Questions Like an Expert

For every tough question, there's an answer
waiting to be unveiled.

Sometimes, you cannot or do not want to give someone all the information on a topic. Being evasive can be useful in these cases. But, maintaining a respectful and sincere demeanor is key. "Evasive" doesn't necessarily mean deceptive, so don't forget to follow up on the points you promise to address later.

Use these techniques ethically and responsibly. If you continually evade questions, your audience may feel misled or frustrated. Balancing these tactics with clear, honest and direct communication whenever possible is crucial.

Answering Difficult Questions

In the landscape of politics and business, successful communication is often a matter of survival. One of the most challenging tests of your skill as a communicator is your ability to handle difficult questions.

The Bridging Technique

'Bridging' allows you to acknowledge the initial query before seamlessly transitioning into a chosen topic or message. Think of it as a bridge you build from their topic to your own.

You use it to control the topic and keep the conversation focused on what you want. This technique is particularly useful during interviews or debates when you might be asked off-topic, controversial, or challenging questions.

How Do You Use It?

Acknowledge the Question:

Start by acknowledging the question the other person has asked you.

If you need time to think, you could say something like,

"That's an interesting question,"

or

"I see why you're asking that."

Next, use a transition phrase to bridge your message.

Examples:

"That's how /not how I see it – going back to…"

"That is a concern, but what our clients tell us they are more concerned about is…"

"I'm not sure about that. What I do know is…"

"That's something we will look into, but what we are concerned with now is…"

"I must say, that's not my experience. When I talk to our stakeholders…"

"People like to say that, but the crucial thing to remember is…"

"I'm afraid I can't speculate on that, but what I can confirm is…"

"That's an interesting point, but I think the bigger issue is…"

"It's too early to talk about that, but we do know the details about X, Y, and Z yet…"

"That is a problem, but the even bigger issue is…"

"That's something we are looking into, but what we are focusing on most is…"

"I'm not sure that's the case. Our research has shown…"

Deliver Your Message:

Now, shift the focus to the topic you want to discuss.

Examples of the Bridging Technique

Question: "Isn't your management team responsible for the current crisis?"

Answer: "I understand your concern. However, we have guided the company through ten years of unprecedented growth. What we need to focus on now is our comprehensive plan to stimulate growth and get the company back on track. The sooner we work together to solve this, the sooner we can return to business as usual. This benefits us all."

Or

Question: "Why has your company's product received negative reviews recently?"

Answer: "I appreciate your concern. But let's remember the hundreds of positive reviews and testimonials from satisfied customers. We focus on providing high-quality products and constantly work on improvements."

Remember always to use the Bridging Technique responsibly and ethically. It should not be used to evade accountability or avoid answering reasonable questions. It's a way for you to steer the conversation, not dodge it entirely.

Training: Bridging Technique Practice

Step 1: Write down three challenging questions you might face in your field. These could be anything you'd prefer not to discuss or topics from which you would like to redirect the focus.

For example:

"Why has your team's performance been declining lately?"

"Can you explain the controversy surrounding your last project?"

"Why haven't you achieved your set targets this quarter?"

Step 2: Write a brief response using the Bridging Technique for each question. Remember the three parts:

a) Acknowledge the question: Start by addressing it without necessarily answering it.

b) Bridge to your message: Use a transition phrase to bridge to the message you want to deliver.

c) Deliver your message: End with a clear and strong statement.

Take your time with each response, ensuring that your transition from the question to your message feels natural and not forced.

Step 3: Practice delivering your responses aloud once you've written them. Pay attention to your tone and ensure a smooth transition to your chosen topic.

This activity should give you a good feel for how the bridging technique works.

Remember, the goal is to keep control over the conversation and guide it in a direction you are comfortable with.

Practice this regularly, and you'll soon be a master of the Bridging Technique.

Deflection: The Artful Dodger

What is the Deflection Technique?

In discussions, our compulsion to answer a direct question is strong, but this often leads to spur-of-the-moment decisions we may regret later. After all, it's often the questions, not the answers, that control the conversation. Mastering the subtle art of deflection allows us to navigate tricky discussions, protect our interests, and leave a favorable impression.

Imagine you're in an interview. The question comes up, "Do you have any other offers?" It's the sort of question that can easily throw us off balance. We've all been there. We're suddenly thrust into a mental gymnastics routine, deciding whether to reveal the truth, which could potentially devalue our offer, or refuse to answer and risk losing trust. Or maybe we consider lying, though that's a high-stakes gamble. There is another option.

Deflection is the art of answering a question with another question, skillfully diverting the conversation back to the questioner.

For instance, in response to "Do you have any other offers?"

You might coyly respond, "Are you planning to make me one?"

Why Use the Deflection Technique?

In human communication, deflection always beats refusal and deception. Why? Because it shows a curiosity to learn instead of an intent to hide information. We're naturally drawn toward people who show openness and curiosity. Therefore, a well-timed deflection can promote trust and likability.

However, the successful implementation of this tactic depends on the context. For example, a subtle deflection might be more easily noticed in larger group scenarios or settings with an audience. Yet, research has shown that the effect is powerful in most one-on-one interactions. This is why top politicians and CEOs worldwide use this technique daily. As with everything, the trick is only to use it when needed and not overdo it.

How Do You Use It?

Acknowledge the Question:

As with most techniques, begin by acknowledging the question.

You could say something like,

"That's an insightful question,"

or "I can see why you're interested in that."

Deflect the Question:

This is where the 'deflection' happens. You could redirect the question back to the questioner or a broader perspective.

How to master the subtle art of deflection:

Firstly, anticipate the tricky questions. Look ahead at those curveballs that might come your way. In an interview, for instance, you might face questions about personal matters, age, or even political beliefs.

Secondly, prepare your deflective counter-questions. Ideally, these should be related to the initial question, maintaining the conversational flow. The best ones prompt the other person to talk about themselves.

Infusing a touch of humor is a masterstroke – it creates a pleasant interaction, steering the conversation gently.

Thirdly, practice makes perfect. Brainstorm possible deflective responses and rehearse them with a friend or colleague. This will better prepare you to navigate those nerve-wracking moments during critical discussions.

Lastly, anticipate the reactions to your deflection. Realize that your question might elicit a direct response from your conversation partner. Be prepared to continue the conversation from there.

Note: Guard yourself against deflection too. If you're the one seeking vital information, note the important questions and pay attention to the responses you receive.

14 Examples of the Deflection Technique

Be careful using these. Always adapt it to the specific conversation, and don't use them if they don't match the situation.

"That's an interesting question. What makes you ask that?"

"Before I answer that, could you share more about why this information is important?"

"I appreciate your curiosity. How do you usually deal with this in your experience?"

"That's an intriguing aspect to consider. What are your thoughts on it?"

"Actually, what's more relevant is... What do you think about that?"

"Well, that's one way to look at it. But have you considered...?"

"There's a story behind that, but I'm more interested in hearing about your perspective."

"What a coincidence that you ask because I was just about to ask you something similar. How would you handle it?"

"I'm curious, what led you to that line of questioning?"

"That's a good point. However, I believe what we should really focus on is... Don't you agree?"

"Let's park that for a moment. I'm really interested in hearing more about your approach to..."

"That's a broad subject. Could we narrow down the focus a bit more?"

"Before we dive into that, could you clarify what you mean by...?"

"You've given me food for thought. In the meantime, I'm wondering about your take on..."

Training: Deflection Technique Practice

Step 1: Identify three potential questions related to your field that you might need help to answer or would rather not answer directly.

They could be something like:

"What's your opinion on the latest controversial policy?"

"Why did you decide to leave your last job?"

"Can you explain why your project didn't meet the deadline?"

Step 2: Craft a response using the Deflection Technique for each question.

a) Acknowledge the question: Show respect for the question asked.

b) Redirect the question: Guide the question back to the asker or a broader issue.

Ensure your response flows smoothly and doesn't feel forced or dismissive.

Step 3: Practice delivering these responses out loud.

Practice, practice, practice!

Remember, the goal of the Deflection Technique isn't to avoid answering all questions but to help you steer the conversation in a comfortable, productive direction. Practice this regularly, and you'll soon master this skill.

So, the next time you're faced with a difficult question, consider not just answering but asking.

Reframing

What is Reframing?

Reframing is a technique to alter a conversation's context or perspective. It's like giving an old painting a brand new frame – the painting (reality) remains the same, but it can look different and provoke a different reaction depending on the frame you choose.

Whether dealing with a challenging client or leading a team meeting, reframing can be your secret weapon to turn the table from negativity to positivity or highlight a unique perspective you think needs attention.

Why is it Useful?

Reframing lets you offer an alternative (but still true) perspective of reality. It allows you to change the narrative without twisting facts.

With it, you can avoid negativity and turn potentially hostile conversations into friendly brainstorming sessions.

It's not about playing mind games but instead about making others see the brighter side of things.

How Do You Use It?

Step 1: Listen and Understand: Listen carefully to the question or statement. Understand its context and the underlying assumptions.

Step 2: Identify the Frame: Determine the speaker's perspective or frame. Are they focusing on a failure, a weakness, a threat, etc.?

Step 3: Decide on a New Frame: Choose a different perspective that could apply to the situation. Think about opportunities instead of threats, strengths instead of weaknesses, and lessons learned rather than battles lost.

Step 4: Communicate Your New Frame: State your reframed perspective confidently and clearly. Authenticity is key here.

Example of Reframing

Original Question: "Why has your team missed its sales targets for the past three months?"

Reframed Response: "True, our targets eluded us these past few months. And this has been a wake-up call for us to analyze and revamp our sales strategy. We've identified vital areas that need fine-tuning, and we can't wait to see the positive results in the coming months."

In the reframed response, you're shifting the focus from missed targets (negative frame) to learning, improving, and the potential for future success (positive frame).

Notice how we've also changed the phrase "we missed our targets" to "our targets have eluded us," changing the focus from what we did wrong to what an outside force, in this case, our targets, have done.

Remember, as you use this tool, be genuine and truthful. Reframing can be perceived as manipulation if not used correctly. You are trying to counter a negative view with a positive view, not deny reality or mislead people.

Exercise: Reframing Technique Practice

In this exercise, you should focus on reframing the statement or question rather than answering it. The objective is to provide you with a new perspective you can discuss in your answer to each.

Task 1:

Original Statement: "Our last marketing campaign was unsuccessful. It didn't generate the expected sales."

Reframe this statement.

Task 2:

Original Question: "Why is our team constantly missing deadlines?"

Reframe this question.

Task 3:

Original Question: "Why has there been such high staff turnover in our department recently?"

Reframe this question.

Answer Key

Below, you will find some possible reframed responses for each task.

It's important to remember that there isn't only one right answer.

It's about changing perspective and focusing on a situation's potential positives or opportunities. You may have provided different answers, and they may also be correct. The exercise is about practicing the shift in perspective.

Task 1:

Reframed Statement: "Our last marketing campaign has provided valuable insights. It has offered a unique chance to understand where we can adjust our approach for better sales."

Task 2:

Reframed Question: "How can we refine our process to better meet project deadlines?"

Task 3:

Reframed Question: "What can we learn from the recent changes in our department's staffing to improve retention in the future?"

Other Techniques

Seeking Clarity: If a question is vague or overly complex, ask for it to be clarified. This gives you additional time to think and can sometimes cause the other person to answer their own question. Say, "Can you clarify what you mean by...?" or "Can you provide a bit more context?"

Postponing the Answer: Politely suggest that the answer would be better given later or after further thought. For instance, "I think that's a significant question that deserves a thoughtful answer, so let me reflect on it and get back to you."

Acknowledging and being Honest When You Don't Know the Answer: Sometimes, it might be best to simply say that you don't know but will find out. "That's a great question. I don't have a specific answer now, but I will certainly look into it." You then follow up on the question once you have researched the answer and can provide some insight. If you think you may not see the person again anytime soon, you can take their details at the end of the class or meeting and get back to them with an answer. People often appreciate this, as it's honest and shows that you care.

Chapter 8. How to Transform Professional Mistakes into Career Victories

In a crisis, it's not the mistake that
defines us; it's how we react.

In our professional lives, the path to success isn't a smooth, straight line. So, how do you maintain your stride and stand tall in times of crisis? The answer lies in how you rise after you fall.

When top international companies and political parties deal with a major scandal, they often use Image Repair Theory. The good news is that now you can use it too.

Perhaps you made a mistake in a crucial project or misspoke in an important meeting. Your professional image and your reputation are at risk. What do you do?

When a crisis arises, you have five strategies that you can use:

Denial

Evasion of Responsibility

Reducing Offensiveness

Corrective Action

Mortification.

Let's look at each individually with examples of how you can phrase it.

Denial: If, for instance, you're blamed for a mistake that wasn't your fault. In this case, denial becomes your shield. You state the facts calmly and assertively, distancing yourself from the error. This isn't about shirking responsibility but making sure others understand the truth. The key is to be clear and assertive yet respectful.

An example could be, "I understand why it might seem like I made this mistake, but upon reviewing the facts, it's clear that I was not involved in this part of the project."

Evasion of Responsibility: Sometimes, factors outside our control lead to negative results. This is where evasion of responsibility comes into play. It's about highlighting those external influences that contributed to the situation, creating a broader context that shows you're not entirely at fault. This isn't an escape hatch; it's a factual explanation.

Here, the focus should be on framing the external factors that led to the problem. It's also a good idea to use the passive voice so you don't indirectly blame yourself or others.

So, instead of saying: "When I made this decision, there were unforeseen circumstances that significantly impacted the outcome. Given the information at hand at the time, the decision that I made seemed appropriate."

You could say, "<u>When this decision was made</u> (passive voice), there were unforeseen circumstances that significantly impacted the outcome. Given the information at hand at the time, the decision seemed appropriate."

Reducing Offensiveness: This is the art of mitigation. When a mistake occurs, you seek to reduce its impact. You might remind your team of your past track record your usually reliable performance, or compare the situation to worse scenarios. It's about reframing the narrative in a way that softens the blow. This is about perspective and context.

You might state, "While I acknowledge the error, it's important to note that in the grand scheme of our project, this is a minor setback and can be quickly rectified. This isn't a pattern; it's a one-off." This can be powerful if you use it correctly. You are showing that you understand that you made a mistake, but you are not exaggerating the importance of the problem.

Corrective Action: Here, we move from defense to offense, pivoting from the problem to the solution. This strategy shows that you have already realized there is a problem and are already taking steps to solve it. It's proactive, it's responsible, and it's powerful. This strategy requires proactivity and commitment to resolution.

An example might be, "I've identified the error and am already working on correcting it. I am also putting measures in place to ensure this doesn't happen in the future."

Mortification: And finally, there's power in humility. This is when you accept your mistake, offer a genuine apology, and express regret. It's about demonstrating emotional intelligence, humility, and the readiness to learn from our errors.

Mortification isn't about showcasing weakness; it highlights strength in vulnerability. Here, humility and sincerity are crucial. You could say, "I take full responsibility for this mistake, and I am truly sorry for the impact it has had. I am committed to learning from this and improving."

Mortification should only be used during a major crisis when it feels like the right action. But if used correctly, this technique can foster incredible respect.

Training 1: Crafting Your Image Repair Response

This exercise will allow you to practice using the abovementioned strategies in hypothetical situations.

Step 1: Imagine three different professional crisis scenarios. Write a brief description of the crisis for each scenario, outlining the key facts.

Example:

1. You've missed an important deadline for a project.

2. You've accidentally shared confidential information in a meeting.

3. Your team's product failed in the market, and you were the team lead.

Step 2: Now, for each crisis scenario, write a short response employing each of the five image repair strategies: Denial, Evasion of Responsibility, Reducing Offensiveness, Corrective Action, and Mortification. You should end up with 15 responses in total.

As you create these responses, refer to the earlier examples and guidelines. Be sure to focus on the language you're using.

Is it clear and respectful?

Are you accurately conveying your intended message?

Step 3: Review each of your responses.

Do they sound sincere and genuine?

Would they potentially mitigate the damage caused by the crisis?

Adjust your responses as necessary for greater impact.

Step 4: Now, reverse roles. Imagine you're a co-worker or manager receiving these responses.

How would you react to each one?

Does the strategy work in diffusing the situation, or does it escalate it further?

Remember, the key to successful image repair is sincerity and taking appropriate responsibility for your actions. This training exercise will help you practice doing just that in different crisis scenarios.

Training 2: Case Study- Turning Career Disasters into Triumphs

A Real-World Case About Using Image Repair for Career Advancement

A few years ago, we worked with a client. For confidentiality, the name 'Adam' has been used in place of his real name throughout this case study.

Adam had built an enviable reputation over the years. His colleagues and subordinates viewed him as the poster child for competence, reliability, and integrity. He was one of the top performers in his department and had aspirations of one day joining the executive team. However, Adam's life was about to be dragged upside down in the blink of an eye.

In an unguarded moment, Adam wrote an email to vent his frustrations about the company's strategic direction, only to accidentally hit 'reply all.' With that click, his inner thoughts were broadcast for everyone to see.

As the email circulated in the office, so did the whispers. Adam's image, carefully constructed over the years, was instantly tarnished. He needed to act fast.

Consideration of Image Repair Strategies

Pause for a second. Think back to the Image Repair Strategies we looked at, at the start of this chapter and answer the following questions:

What should Adam have done in this situation?

What would you do?

Write down a rough action plan before you continue reading this case study.

Are you ready to continue reading? Let's go.

Consultation and Assessment

When Adam came to see me, he was so distraught that he considered quitting his job and changing careers.

Adam was almost in tears when he walked into my office that day. I felt for him. His usual air of confidence was replaced with an aura of panic.

"I'm thinking of quitting," he confessed after explaining what had happened. I felt the utter desperation in his voice.

"Quitting might seem like the easy way out, Adam, but it's not your only option. Let's remember that you're facing a crisis, not a catastrophe," I gently suggested, reminding him of the value he had brought to his company over the years.

"Easy for you to say. My professional reputation is ruined," Adam countered, his frustration clear.

"Is it? Or does it just feel that way right now?" I prodded, aiming to shift his perspective. "Remember, Adam, the essence of Image Repair isn't about erasing mistakes. It's about turning them into opportunities for growth. This isn't the end of your journey; it's a tough curve in the road."

I took a moment to breathe while I looked at Adam. What would I do if I were him? I'd be standing exactly where he was.

He looked at me expectantly as if he was hoping that I would produce some magical solution that would make it all go away.

"Adam," I started, "let's set a goal for this session. What would you like to have achieved when we leave here today?" My question took his mind away from the problem and toward a solution, at least for a moment.

Adam seemed unsure, "I guess I want you to help me solve this. I love my job, and I don't want to quit."

"That's a fair starting point, Adam. Let's get more specific. Are we talking about managing the immediate damage, looking at long-term reputation repair, or both?"

Adam pondered on this. "Both, I think. Yes, both."

"Good. Now, let's examine the reality of the situation. You've sent an email unintentionally that's created a stir. What are the consequences so far?"

Adam looked uncomfortable, "People are talking. They are questioning my judgment, and I feel I've lost their respect."

Exploring Image Repair Strategies

Over the next few hours, we explored Adam's options. First, we looked at Denial. Was this a valid option? It quickly became apparent that it wasn't - the email was out there, and denying it would only make matters worse.

Next, we examined the possibility of Evasion of Responsibility. Could Adam blame external factors for his actions? While there was some truth to his frustration with the company's strategic direction, it was clear that the action was driven more by Adam's momentary lapse in judgment than by any external circumstance.

The third option, Reducing Offensiveness, had potential. Adam could highlight his otherwise sterling reputation and compare this incident to other, more serious issues. But this strategy required careful handling; overdoing it could make him seem dismissive of the severity of his mistake.

We considered Corrective Action - Adam acknowledging his mistake and taking proactive steps to fix the situation. He could ask the IT department to retract the email, issue an apology, and suggest a company-wide discussion about the issues he'd raised in his email. This showed promise.

Finally, we evaluated Mortification. Adam would have to accept his mistake, offer a sincere apology, and express regret. This would be challenging, as Adam was naturally introverted and uncomfortable being emotionally vulnerable in front of others.

Taking Action and the Outcome

Adam swiftly issued an apology email, expressing his remorse for the incident and acknowledging that his words were inappropriately harsh and not reflective of the company's strategy.

The second part of his strategy involved corrective action. This is where you promise to fix the situation and ensure it does not happen again. Adam took this route by scheduling an open forum meeting, allowing everyone to express their thoughts and concerns regarding the company's direction more professionally and constructively.

Conclusion: Lessons and Impact

So, what can we learn from Adam's story?

Well, two things stand out.

First, none of us are immune to mistakes. We all, at some point, stumble and risk our professional image. What matters is how we handle these situations. Adam chose to own his mistake, and through his humility and proactive response, he salvaged his reputation and even managed to turn a crisis into an opportunity for open dialogue.

Second, image repair isn't just about correcting a mistake or making one grand gesture. It's about consistent action over time. Adam's open forum wasn't a one-time event. It became a regular occurrence, showing his team that he was serious about promoting transparency and improving communication.

Ultimately, this mishap didn't mark the end of Adam's career. Instead, it became a critical turning point. By embracing the image repair strategies in this chapter, Adam managed to weather the storm, restoring his reputation and even deepening the trust and respect of his colleagues.

Reflection

As Adam showed us, Image Repair is more than a theoretical concept – it's a practical tool that can help us navigate the unpredictable waters of the professional world. And as we have learned repeatedly, it's not the absence of mistakes that defines us, but our actions in the face of them.

By applying Image Repair in your personal and professional communication, you are setting a beacon for others. You're saying, "Look, I'm human. I messed up. But watch how I learn from it and ensure it doesn't happen again."

As the saying goes: "No publicity is bad publicity." It's an opportunity to display character, strength, humility, and resilience. It can turn what might have been a damaging incident into a compelling narrative of growth and redemption. Just like Adam did, you might find that you have gained an enormous amount of respect and trust when the storm is over. To end this case study, I will add that Adam managed to become a C-level executive. Two years later, he was promoted to Chief Marketing Officer.

Discussion

1. Imagine you are a colleague who received Adam's email. How would you react?

   And later, how would your view change after his apology and the implementation of his corrective action?

   What key elements in Adam's actions influenced your perspective?

2. Role-play an alternative scenario: Adam chose Denial or Evasion of Responsibility strategies instead of Corrective Action and Mortification.

   How could these choices have played out in the office environment?

   What might have been the potential impact on Adam's reputation and the company culture?

3. Imagine you are Adam. Draft an alternative apology speech that still uses the strategies of Corrective Action and Mortification. If possible, share your draft with someone else and explain your choices in tone, wording, and the specific corrective actions you propose.

Thank You

Dear Reader,

First and foremost, thank you for joining us on this journey!

In the next few pages, we've compiled an essential Resource Library to further improve your understanding and application of the concepts discussed. These resources have been meticulously selected to provide deeper insights and practical tools for professionals just like you.

We genuinely hope you enjoyed the experience as much as we enjoyed bringing it to life for you.

If this book was helpful, please take a moment to leave a review on Amazon or Audible.

PS: Don't forget to sign up for our **Free Executive Club,** where you will get access to a range of top training materials, templates, books, and courses.

Best Regards,

Marc

marc@macsonbell.com

It's 100% free for you: **https://www.macsonbell.com/free-toolbox-sign-up-form**

5 Expert Breathing Techniques for Effective Speaking

https://www.macsonbell.com/post/5-expert-breathing-techniques-for-effective-speaking

The 7 Communication Habits of Highly Effective Teams

https://www.macsonbell.com/post/7-business-communication-habits-of-highly-effective-teams

Active Listening Techniques

Access this digital resource here:
https://www.macsonbell.com/active-listening

PRIVATE LIBRARY ACCESS

Get the FREE books here:

https://www.macsonbell.com/free-toolbox-sign-up-form

Executive Communication Club

Sign up for our FREE Executive Communication Club training emails and private library access!

Get your **FREE Access Pass** here:

https://www.macsonbell.com/free-toolbox-sign-up-form

Thank you for reading.

349 Expert Speaking Templates, Phrases & Idioms for Professional Communication in English

https://www.macsonbell.com/free-toolbox-sign-up-form

About the Author

MARC ROCHE is a Language Specialist, Executive Communication Coach, and best-selling author. Before setting up Macson Bell Training, Marc worked as an Academic Writing, Business Communication, and Legal English Trainer for organizations like the British Council, the Royal Melbourne Institute of Technology, and the University of Technology Sydney. Marc has also delivered corporate training within multinationals such as Nike, GlaxoSmithKline, and Bolsas y Mercados, among many others.

He studied Business Management & Business Law at university before gaining his teaching qualification, and he is currently completing an MBA.

Marc is originally from the UK, and in his free time, he likes to travel, cook, write, play sports, watch football, and spend time with friends and family.

Learn more about Marc at amazon.com/author/marcroche

FREE training resources for students and teachers: **https://www.macsonbell.com/free-toolbox-sign-up-form**

Printed in Great Britain
by Amazon

53267973R00072